Work from Home:
How to Build a Successful Online Business

Learn How to Start An Online Business For FREE:
www.lacobizonlinebusiness.com

© **Copyright 2016 by LacoBiz - All rights reserved.**

This document is geared towards providing exact and reliable information in regards to the topic and issue covered. The publication is sold with the idea that the publisher is not required to render accounting, officially permitted, or otherwise, qualified services. If advice is necessary, legal or professional, a practiced individual in the profession should be ordered.

- From a Declaration of Principles which was accepted and approved equally by a Committee of the American Bar Association and a Committee of Publishers and Associations.

In no way is it legal to reproduce, duplicate, or transmit any part of this document in either electronic means or in printed format. Recording of this publication is strictly prohibited and any storage of this document is not allowed unless with written permission from the publisher. All rights reserved.

The information provided herein is stated to be truthful and consistent, in that any liability, in terms of inattention or otherwise, by any usage or abuse of any policies, processes, or directions contained within is the solitary and utter responsibility of the recipient reader. Under no circumstances will any legal responsibility or blame be held against the publisher for any reparation, damages, or monetary loss due to the information herein, either directly or indirectly.

Respective authors own all copyrights not held by the publisher.

The information herein is offered for informational purposes solely, and is universal as so. The presentation of the information is without contract or any type of guarantee assurance.

Learn How to Start An Online Business For FREE:
www.lacobizonlinebusiness.com

The trademarks that are used are without any consent, and the publication of the trademark is without permission or backing by the trademark owner. All trademarks and brands within this book are for clarifying purposes only and are the owned by the owners themselves, not affiliated with this document.

Table of Contents

INTRODUCTION 6

CHAPTER ONE: WHAT IS AFFILIATE MARKETING? 7

CHAPTER TWO: THE ROAD MAP TO SUCCESS 9

CHAPTER THREE: NOT A "GET RICH FAST" SCHEME 12

CHAPTER FOUR: WHY IT IS THE PERFECT TIME TO START WITH AFFILIATE MARKETING 14

CHAPTER FIVE: THE BENEFITS OF AFFILIATE MARKETING 16

CHAPTER SIX: MONETIZING YOUR SITE 19

CHAPTER SEVEN: WRITING QUALITY CONTENT 24

CHAPTER EIGHT: KEYWORD RESEARCH 32

CHAPTER NINE: SEOS 37

CHAPTER TEN: BUILDING YOUR EMAIL LIST 40

CHAPTER ELEVEN: REGISTERING A DOMAIN NAME AND MAINTAINING IT . 44

CHAPTER TWELVE: ENGAGING READERS 49

CONCLUSION 52

Learn How to Start An Online Business For FREE:
www.lacobizonlinebusiness.com

WAIT!!! Before you go on and read my book. I would like to thank you for downloading this book. I also want to share with you my own experience and how to start a successful online business from scratch.

Are you tired of not know what to do or where to begin? Please visit my website and I'll share with you everything I know, just follow the link below:

www.lacobizonlinebusiness.com

Introduction

Congratulations on downloading *Work from Home* and thank you for doing so.

The following chapters will discuss how you are going to have the choice of working from home doing Affiliate Marketing. You can take what you learn in this book and apply it to pretty much any business.

There are plenty of books on this subject on the market, thanks again for choosing this one! Every effort was made to ensure it is full of as much useful information as possible, please enjoy!

Chapter one: What is Affiliate Marketing?

Affiliate marketing is known as a type of marketing that is performance based. The business is going to reward each affiliate for every visitor or even every customer that was brought to the company by the affiliates marketing efforts.

There are going to be four players when you look at affiliate marketing. The merchant which is also the retailer or the brand that the affiliate is trying to sell. The network which will contain the offers that the affiliate is going to choose from. It is also going to take care of the payments that are sent in. the publisher or the affiliate who is doing the selling. And the customer who is doing the buying of what the affiliate is selling.

The market is very complex and is going to create a second tier of employees who are going to be included. This second tier is affiliate management agencies, specialized third party vendors, and super affiliates.

Internet marketing and affiliate marketing are will have overlapping methods since affiliates tend to use some of the more recognized advertising methods.

Many methods that are used are organic search engine optimization, email marketing, content marketing, paid search engine marketing, and display advertising. But, there are also some affiliates that turn to methods that are less orthodox like publishing reviews or services that are be offered by some of their partners.

You can also see affiliate marketing is tied to referral marketing because these forms of marketing are going to use third parties to drive up sales from the retailers. But, you will find that they have some differences between them. The primary difference is that affiliate marketing is going to rely on financial desire while referral marketing is built on trust and personal relationships.

Affiliate marketing tends to get overlooked by advertisers. But, email, search engines, and website syndication so that they can capture online retailer's attention. Affiliate marketing is going to have a lower profile, but it still has a major role when looking at marketing strategies that e-retailers use.

The whole concept of affiliate marketing came from revenue sharking which goes well beyond the internet. The translation for revenue share principles became mainstream to e-commerce in November 1994. This was almost four years after the internet came around.

Affiliate marketing on the internet was thought and put into practice by William J. Tobin who is the founder of PC Flowers and Gifts. Later, it was launched onto the Prodigy Network in 1989 by PC Flowers and Gifts which was in service until '96. But in '93 PC Flowers and Gifts ended up generating sales that surpassed six million a year for the Prodigy service. However, in 1998 PC Flowers and Gifts could develop a business model that showed how they were going to pay the commission on the sales that were created on the Prodigy network.

Chapter two: The Road Map to Success

Every good business is going to have a plan that will include how they plan to succeed. Affiliate marketing from home is no different. You can be successful and have a large commission from the sales you make with your chosen retailer.

Unique

As an affiliate, you have the ability to offer whatever you desire to sell should you have the proper platform to promote it. But, that is where most affiliates go wrong. They try to oversell anything that people can buy. But, the quick tip to being successful to find something unique to offer to your customers. It will be easier to focus all of your attention on a specific niche rather than trying to scatter your efforts over several different products or services.

Search Engine Marketing

After you have become an affiliate, your job is to promote a service or product. There are a great majority of affiliates that end up using a pay per click engine. But, it will be more beneficial if you learn how to use organic search results. Doing this is going to help to save you money since you will be spending a lot of it when it comes to pay per click engines. You should only use pay per click engines when you have knowledge of what you are doing to avoid overspending.

Your product and your audience

You should be a fountain of knowledge when it comes to what good or service you are offering. The more information you have, the more credibility you are going to have. The credibility you build is going to build trust with your audience. When your audience does not trust you, they most likely will not want to purchase anything from you.

Multiple products

While you should have a unique niche, you should have multiple products to offer. Have multiple products is going to help you when it comes to a product that is not selling despite your best efforts to promote it and get it sold. It will also give you several lines of income.

Embrace change

With the internet constantly changing, it is will not be the same as it was a couple months ago. So, the strategies that you were using back then may not work now. Be sure to stay on top of trends so that you can keep your promotion skills up to par and sell your products. Learn something new about your job every day, this is going to help you when it comes to learning the new ways that you can promote the product. If you are seeking that super affiliate title, you have to be willing spend time learning and embracing the changes that come with internet marketing.

Never give up

Promoting product to the proper crowd is hard, and a lot of the time there are people who just dip their toes into affiliate marketing before giving up. But, if you monitor your statistics, you are going to see what techniques works and what does not. This is going to help you in changing your plans so that you are able to do what works and not worry about the things that do not work. Make the changes that are necessary to keep yourself on top of your game. Being patient and consistent are going to be a big must when it comes to affiliate marketing. But, at the end of the day it is going to end up paying off.

Affiliate marketing does not happen overnight. You must be persistent, knowledgeable, patient, and grow and develop as the internet changes.

Chapter three: Not a "Get Rich Fast" Scheme

Everyone is leery of working from home because there are so many companies out there that are schemes that promise to make you rich quick. But, affiliate marketing is not one such scheme that we see so often.

If you do affiliate marketing correcting, you are going to make money, but you are not going to get rich quick. Unlike the get rich quick schemes, affiliate marketing is going to only make you money based on how much work you devote to it.

As mentioned before, affiliate marketing is about making relationships with your retailers and customers. Building the proper relationship and having the trust that your retailer and customer needs to have in you is going be the start to your journey, just like promoting and selling the good or service that you have selected.

When trying to make money doing affiliate marketing, you have to stay focused on your goal. You may not be getting a ton of money yet, but you cannot give up just because of that. Keep testing out what you think is going to work and eventually you are going to locate the perfect plan that works.

There will be periods where you will lose money. That is another way to know that this is not a scheme where you are going to get rich quick. During your tough periods, learn more about your products. And develop new strategies. Sooner or later you are going to end up making money.

Set goals, the only way you are going to be successful is if you try. Reaching your goals is a great way for you to feel as if you have achieved something.

Let's look at two different situations.

Situation one: how long do you consider to be quick?

Everyone measures time differently. To some a week is quick, to others two years is quick. Depending on your concept of time, is going to depend on if you think affiliate marketing is a get rich quick scheme. But, if you have the notion that you are going to get rich, instantly you are wrong.

Situation two: if you think that you can get rich and not put in the time that is needed to do the proper marketing. Then affiliate marketing is defiantly not a get rich quick scheme.

Affiliate marketing is going to take a lot of time and research on your part. You will need to create promotion platforms, learn what affiliated marketing is, select your niche, and so much more.

Affiliate marketing requires a lot of effort on your part, it will not do the work for you by just allowing you to lounge at home on the couch. Not to mention you are need to be dedicated if you have a desire to make any money.

When someone tries to tell you that affiliate marketing is a get rich quick scheme, they are attempting to sell their own product amongst people that attempt to get into the market. There are going to be some exceptions, but there are only going to be a handful of people that become rich.

Chapter four: Why It Is the Perfect Time to Start with Affiliate Marketing

At some point in time you have looked at working online so that you can stay at home. Perhaps you looked at affiliate marketing and thought that maybe you could do it, but you were not sure if you should or not.

When you look at what people are saying about affiliate marketing, you will discover that some people are saying that it is dead. But, this is far from the truth. The real truth is that many affiliates are dropping out because they are not making the chunk of change that they want to be making. But, the money that is there to earn is the exact same as it always has been. Ultimately, it means that people who are getting out of affiliate marketing are not serious about making money. But, the great news is that the money they are passing up, is still there for those who are serious about making money.

Every day that passes, the tools and technology that is available to you is getting better and faster than ever. Nowadays there are trackers such as Thrive or Voluum as well as spy tools like WhatRunsWhere and BoxofAds. Not just that, but there are more choices as to how you can make a paycheck online, the biggest thing that you need to understand is that tracking and optimizing is important.

Once, again, thanks to modern technology, you are able to track everything with the push of a button.

With networks being faster, you are no longer paid on a NET30 basis as an affiliate. So, any money that you make in June will be paid out at the end of July, maybe the beginning of August. Any business that focuses solely on their cash flow is going to end up being a deadly business. Looking at things now, networks can payout weekly and on better terms than ever before. Even though you should not focus on money, it does have some major pull when it comes to keeping your traffic flow steady.

Unlike five or ten years ago, asking for help has gotten easier. It used to be that if you ever asked anyone about affiliated marketing, you would get charged a lot, or you would get an answer that was not going to be very helpful. But, now people are going to be more open to ensuring that you get the help that you need.

Some of the more successful affiliates are going to give advice on blogs that they have started in order to help other affiliates out who are just starting or who are having a hard time making a go of it. However, the help does not stop there. You can also go to web forums that will provide you with the information that you are seeking as well.

Some sites offer training that you can pay for. It is going to cost you small monthly fee, but you are going to have access to take classes from multiple people that have become successful. And, do not worry about the money that you are having to put out for a membership, you are most likely going to earn it back in a month or two.

Even if you still have doubts, the time to join affiliate marketing is going to be now! The market is just right and you can probably be able to pick up on some of the products that previous affiliates have dropped because they did not make the money that they wanted, or they thought that it was too hard for them to continue.

Do your research, but know that affiliate marketing is going to one of the correct options for you to get into when you are researching your options for working from home.

Learn How to Start An Online Business For FREE:
www.lacobizonlinebusiness.com

Chapter five: The Benefits of Affiliate Marketing

Affiliate marketing has its major benefits! There are so many reasons as to why you are going to want to consider affiliate marketing that it is not even funny. You may not have known about these benefits before because sometimes they tend to get lost amongst the details of what affiliate marketing actually is and the fact that it is not a get quick rich scheme.

But, now is when we are going to discuss what the benefits are when it comes to affiliate marketing.

Cost effective

Affiliate marketing is going to be cost effective because you are not having to travel somewhere in order to work. Not only that, but it is not going to require you to spend that much money for you to start out.

While affiliate marketing is going to demand that you have an abundance of patience and put in a lot of dedication to making sure that it operates that way you are can save money to start out rather than spend it.

Global market

It does not matter where you are located, you are going to be able to reach out across the world with the goods and services that you are attempting to sell. All because of the internet. You can be living in the Central United States and be trying to promote product in New Zealand!

No fees

There are no fees to join an affiliate program. Many companies are going to allow you to become an affiliate with them just so that you can promote what they are trying to sell.

No storage

You are not going to have to worry about inventory because you are not actually selling the product. You are sending a customer to the company so that they can purchase the product for themselves. So, the merchant is going to maintain the inventory.

No shipping

Along with not having to deal with inventory, you are not going to have to send out the product since you are not dealing with it. Not having to deal with shipping costs is going to save you some money too!

Passive income

Affiliate marketing is a passive income because it does not take much for you to start making money doing it. Yes, it does take you doing a lot of investigating so that you are able to locate the proper platforms to promote the goods that you are wanting to be affiliated with. Because of how technology is, you are going to earn an income from affiliate marketing every week in just a couple of hours a day.

Work from home

Because affiliate marketing is internet based, you can do it from home! All you need to have is a computer, internet access, and the capacity to dedicate the time that is required to make sure that you can promote the goods adequately, you are going to be able to work wherever you want to.

Financial freedom

With affiliate marketing being low cost and able to be done anywhere, you are going to be able to earn your financial freedom through affiliate marketing. It has been said that you are going to have the capacity to make more doing affiliate marketing than you can if you work at a nine to five job every day.

Chapter six: Monetizing Your Site

When you start affiliate marketing, you are going to need platforms where you have the ability to push your product that you have chosen. Most of the time, you are going to use a blog so that you can write reviews on your items or to post various things about it.

To make money off of the site that you pick to use, you are going to need to be able to find ways to make money off of it. This does not necessarily mean that you have to litter your blog with ads if that is the platform you are using. There are other ways that you can make money off your site without overwhelming your users with ads.

Write what you know

Even if you are not an expert on the product that you are selling, you should write what you know about it. Try the product out and see what you can write about it.

Chances are that you have already chosen a niche for your affiliate marketing, and eventually you are going to end up being an expert on it the longer that you sell it. This is not a bad thing! The more knowledge that you have the more methods you are going to be able to use to promote it.

You are not going to have a shortage of resources that you are going to be able to fall back on when it comes to writing about your product. Just commit to writing and people will come to read what you are posting and possibly even buy the product that you are trying to sell.

Learn from the best

As it was said earlier, you can find blogs from other affiliates to learn tips on what you should be doing. When you are reading their blog, you are going to be able to figure out what they do to make their products better known and sell.

If you need to, you can always contact affiliates that have been doing it longer than you and see if they have any advice that they can give you that they may not have put online for everyone else to see.

Having a mentor is not a bad thing, it is actually going to help you out when it comes to learning the ropes of affiliate marketing.

Training

There are multiple training curriculum that you are going to be able to find and attend online. One is Wealthy Affiliate and it is not just a training course, but a community as well for you to network and find people to help you.

Training platforms are going to help you to build your business up from the ground by giving you detailed courses that are designed especially for beginners.

An added bonus is that classes like Wealthy Affiliate will provide a complete solution for anything that you are going to need to learn with affiliate marketing.

Marketing is not selling

Whenever you go online to try and locate a product, you may discover that there are a dozen different results that you find with people trying to sell you a product that they have become affiliated to.

The sad thing is that many affiliates forget what affiliate marketing really is.

A business of helping, not selling

You should always try and help any potential customer so that they can make an educated purchase. You should try and bridge any benefits and features of the product to a real life example, and you should always trust the author.

All three of those points are going to give you the basis for a great customer review.

Focus on traffic from SEOs

Search engines are the most effective way to get target traffic. This is because people use search engines for everything. And, the better you are ranked with the keywords you use for search engines, the more profit you are going to be able to have.

Keyword searches are going to be the core of an SEO if you are able to master SEOs, then you are going to be on the correct path to making a profile online.

SEO tools

When you are using SEOs you should use tools to help you to find the proper keywords to that are going to be unique and bring you a lot of traffic.

Different affiliate promotion formats

The best way to promote any product is to give honest reviews of it. However, there are multiple ways that you are going to be able to put a review on your blog that will include various objects that your clients want to know.

Product reviews

As mentioned before, a product review is the number one way to attract customers. In your review, you should list any pros and cons of the product.

The number one thing is to be completely honest. People look at reviews and typically base their purchases on if the review was any good or not. If you genuinely did not like the product, then do not hide that when you are writing your review, but do not just say that you do not like the product, explain why you did not like it to your customers.

One thing that a lot of reviews often forget is how you can tell your friends to use the product. If you include this, you are more likely to get some more people to purchase the wares that you are promoting.

Your review should always include:

- Targeted keywords in the headline
- Your affiliated link
- Your recommendation
- Your experience with the product.

Resource page

People are always searching for ways to make their lives easier and optimize their time. If you put a page together that has all of your personal tools and resources, then you are sharing resources with your readers can use to make their life easier.

Comparison and top tens

Just like review posts, you are going to be reviewing product; but, you will be reviewing multiple products. After you have reviewed them, you are going to put them into a series of the best product to the worst so that your readers can see what your opinion on all of them was.

If you want something other than a list, then a versus post works just as well. As long as you are taking two different items that happen to be somewhat similar and compare them so that you can tell your readers the difference.

Tutorials

One method that is going to drive sales up is if you take the time to put together tutorials on how customers can use the product that you are trying to sell. It is going to take you a while to put the perfect tutorial together, but it is going to help you later on.

By creating a post that is going to show someone each step on how they can accomplish something, you are going to be giving the product or service one extra key component.

Chapter seven: Writing Quality Content

What you write about the products or services that you are trying to sell is going to make or break your sale. It is vitally important that when you are writing you are writing content that is quality so that your readers are enticed to buy what you are trying to promote.

For some, quality content is easy, but for others it is going to be hard because writing is not a natural skill for them. But, even if you have been writing your entire life, you still have more to learn about writing quality content.

The saying that practice makes perfect is true, the more time that is spent practicing writing, the better you are going to get at writing content that captures your readers attention and entices them into buying almost anything.

Your own unique voice

When you are writing, it is easy to try and imitate others because we think that they are better writers than we are. However, that is not going to attract readers, nor will it help to sell product. You need to write unique content that is in your own voice.

It takes a while to locate your own voice, and even when you do, it is going to continue to need to be developed so that you can hone your skills. Style is one of the single most important tools that writer of any sort needs to have. And, as you continue in your career, it should continue to evolve as you mature.

Ernest Hemingway said: "We are all apprentices in a craft where no one ever becomes a master. "

You should never try to copycat another author's voice, if you copy their voice, then you are never going to find your own voice and people are not going connect with you and what you are writing since they do not know the real you.

To try and find your own voice, you should find a couple of writers that have a style that you enjoy to read. After you have done that, select a single piece of theirs that you think truly represents their voice.

Once you have selected the writing samples, you are going to need to read through it slowly and study how the author caused their voice to come through. Whenever you think that you have gotten it down, you should try and do it yourself. Write a small sample so that you can create your own brand that is similar but not the exact same as the one that you like.

You are going to need to do this with every author and article that you picked. By the end of going through all of them you should have around five articles that you have written that are going to be similar to the ones that you read. At this point in time, you should review what you have written and find the one that sounds the most like you. If you do not feel like any of them sound like you, try to combine the different styles.

Tweak your writing until you have found the one the you like most and that sounds the most like you.

Stay on topic

You should only have one point that you are trying to get across in your writing. And when you are writing about that topic, you need to stay on topic and do not write about something random in the middle of your post.

Whenever you have finished your post. Go back and edit to be sure that you stayed on point. Anywhere that you have gotten off point needs to be erased from your writing because it is only going to lead to confusing your reader about what you are trying to tell them.

Depth and length

Two of the hardest things to deal with when you are writing is depth and length. If they are not perfect, then your writing is going to be difficult to read. You can end up not giving enough detail about what you are trying to tell your author, while you only give them a fraction of the information that they want. Or, you can end up giving them too much information and not have enough space to fill it in.

Your depth needs to match the length of your writing. If you are writing short posts, then you need to give enough detail that it is going to cover all the details that you want in the article. But, do not overload it with detail because then you are only going to end up confusing your reader and they are not going to know what your point was.

Angles

No matter what kind of post that you are writing you should have a topic, point, and slant to your writing.

Your topic needs to be what you are trying to get across to your reader. The slant is will be the unique and specific point of view that is only going to come from you. Finally, the point is going to be the major idea that will take up a majority of what you are writing about.

Do not repeat things that you have already said because you are going to end up not having enough room for your main points. Find a unique way to talk about things so that people see your point of view, not one that they have seen a million times before.

Title

Your title needs to have as much thought put into it as the main body of your post. Your title needs to draw your readers in so that they feel like they want to read what you have written. Not just that, but you should forecast the information that can be read in your post so that it is not a big surprise as to what you are writing about.

Some of the types of tiles that are going to do well are:

- Secrets of....
- Number of....
- Breaking news
- Top #....
- Newsjacking
- How to....
- Interview with....
- Best of....

First sentence

Whenever a reader has decided to read what you have written, you have about three seconds to get them to keep reading before they decide to put it down. The first sentence is going to be the headline for what you are writing about.

Do not mislead with your first sentence. If you are writing about the worst product that you have ever experienced, do not put that it is the best product in the world. In doing that, the reader is going to think that you are telling them something about a product that they are going to want to buy rather than telling them that they should not buy it.

An irresistible lead

The lead is going to be your introduction to your content. For your shorter posts, it is going to be in the first paragraph or two, but if you creating a longer post, it is going to be in the first hundred to six hundred words.

Your point needs to be compelling but not so long that it causes your readers to lose interest. Think of your lead like a teaser as to what is going to come for your readers, but do not let them know what you are going to put in your post later on or else you are just going to be repeating information that they have already read.

Some of the best leads are:

- Breaking news
- Stories (that pertain to what you are writing about)
- Promises of information that cannot be found anywhere else
- Facts that are not well known
- Contrarian viewpoints

Keep it believable

If your facts are not true then no one is going to want to read what you have to write. So, do not stretch the truth. Do not add in any hype either.

Hype tends to cause people to feel as if they have been manipulated which no one is going to like and then they are not going to read what you have to write about the product that you are promoting. Not just that, but you are going to lose other potential customers because they are not going to tell their friends or their family about the product.

Only write content that is going to aid someone in deciding if they are wanting to purchase the product that you are affiliated with. Use a sales copy that is going to help you sell along with content that is going to inspire them about the product.

Do not stretch the truth. If people can trust you, they are only going to use you as a resource to buy the product if they can trust you. So, do research on the products that you are affiliated with. Know all aspects that there are to know about the product and then some, you should know more about the product than your customer does.

Anything that you put into the content of your post, you should be able to back it up using a reliable source. If you get your information off of the company website, then you need to put your source into your post. Add links to any quotes that you get off of other people or books that you have used for research.

It should be easy for people to believe what you are saying or they are not going to be interested in your product.

Closing

Any good content is going to tell you, who, what, when, where, why, and how. But, it is also going to tell your reader, so what. Your content should not lose steam due to the fact that you have run out of ideas on what you want to include in your post.

Whenever you go to close out your content, you need to summarize what your main point was. Your readers need to know that they are going to benefit from the information that you gave them and hopefully have convinced them to buy the product or service you are promoting.

If you can you should always try and bring your main point back to the closing so that everything is tied up neatly.

Plain writing

The shorter the paragraph and sentence, the more readable it is going to be. Do not try and write long sentences that have words that are going to cause people to need to rush to the dictionary so that they can find the definition of a word that you have used. Doing that is only going to cause a reader to drop what they are reading because they are not going to want to cause they do not want to have to work hard to read something.

Keep it simple. Think of it like this:

- Each word should be one to two syllables.
- Each sentence should have about twenty-five words
- And each paragraph should be six lines

If you cannot fit in your product promotion in that small amount of space, then you need to relook at what you have written and cut out what is not going to be needed.

Edit!

Do not publish the first draft of what you have written about your product. The first draft is going to be where you try and get all of your ideas out and in the proper order using the right words. If you do not like your first draft, then you are among the many writers who hate their first draft.

Your draft is going to get better after you have edited it. But, just because you are going to edit all of your posts does not mean that you should not try to get all of your ideas out. Write fast so that all of your ideas get out so that you do not have to worry about forgetting what you are wanting to say about your product. Whenever you are editing, you need to put your best effort in so that you end up with the best copy of your post.

You may go through several different edits before you find the high quality that you are looking for before you post your promotions.

Chapter eight: Keyword Research

For anyone to find your blog or website with the products or services that you are affiliated with, they are going to go to a search engine and type in the proper series of words to find you.

Keyword research is vitally important for anyone who is wanting to get found on the internet. Keyword research is also going to give you a high return when it comes to the searches. The rankings on every keyword that you decide to use is going to either make or break the site that you create. So, by researching the keywords that are in high demand in your market, you are going to learn which terms and phrases will do you best so that they can be targeted by an SEO while giving you insight to your customers.

While getting people to visit your site is good, but you do not just want anyone to visit your site, you want the right kind of people to visit your site so that they are going to be more likely to buy what you are trying to promote. Having insight to potential customers is going to be key so that you are able to find the proper keywords that are going to get them to you.

Keyword research is going to help to predict the shifts in demand as the market changes while you promote your product or service. This is going to tie directly into what people are looking for on the web.

The value of keywords

How much value does one particular keyword hold to your website? For example, if you are affiliated with history books, are you wanting people to come to your site whenever they are trying to locate Chinese history or Greek history? They keywords that someone types into a search engine are going to be available to a webmaster. But, tools that will aid in keyword research are going to help you to locate this information so that it can better benefit you.

The downside is going to be that these tools will not show you just how valuable all of the traffic to your site truly is because of these searches. So, when trying to understand the value of keywords, you first must understand your own site. You should make a hypotheses, test it, and repeat until you find the proper keywords that bring the right customers to you.

In trying to assess a keywords value you are going to want to:

- Figure out if the keyword is even relevant to what your website contains. Is that keyword going to bring people who are looking for history books? Or do you need to narrow down your keywords so that it is more specific. If you are promoting only Greek history, you do not want someone who wants to know about the history of the Native Americans. Is the keyword that you have chosen going to satisfy the needs of your reader's search? Is the proper audience coming to your site so that you are able to see financial rewards? If you can say yes to everything, then you have passed step one and are now able to move on to assessing your keyword.

- At this point in time, you are going to want to take the phrases or words that you have chosen and search for them in all of the major search engines. Doing this is going to help you to understand exactly how the keywords that you picked are ranked and how valuable they are. Not just that, but you can see who is going to be your competition. What kind of advertisements are sponsored by the words or phrases that you have entered? The more ads that pop up, the more valuable the word typically is. If more ads appear above an organic result, the word is going to be very lucrative and directly conversion prone.

- Buy a campaign sample for the keyword of choice with AdWords or AdCenter. If you cannot locate your website when you do your searches, then you are going to be able to buy a campaign and test how much traffic is able to see your site based on the keywords that you have chosen. Adwords is going to give you an exact match along with pointing the appropriate traffic of the pages of your site. From here you will have the capabilities to track your conversion rates and impressions for every two hundred to three hundred clicks.

- With the information that you have now collected, you are going to be able to determine exactly how valuable every one of your keywords are. If you assume that your search is able to generate seven thousand impressions in a single day, where fifty of those visitors come to your site, and two of them actually buy the product that you are affiliated with, then the keyword is going to be worth the number of sales you make. So, if you make five hundred dollars off of two visitors, then that word is worth five dollars.

Long tail of keyword demand

Sticking with the history book example, how awesome would it be if you could be the number one ranked site when it comes to history books? You would get all of the sales because people would come to your site first!

If your keywords are able to have seven thousand searches in a day, or even if they earn seven hundred in a day you are doing well. However, if you look at things realistically, being popular based on the search is only going to make up a small percentages of the searches that are done across the internet. The remaining percent is going to be called "long tail" of the search.

Long tail typically contains thousands of searches that are conducted any any given point in the day. These searches can be done a few times a day and when looked at together, they are going to comprise a large portion of the search volume around the world.

Marketers have come to know that long tail keywords are going to convert better since people are caught in a buying/conversion cycle later on. When a person searches for history books, they are simply browsing to see what they can find and not really looking to buy. On the other hand, when someone is searching specifically for Greek history books, they are looking to buy and you are going to want them to buy from you!

When you are able to understand the search demand curve, you will see that the amount of queries that will send you a massive amount of traffic. The terms that are less searches will be able to show you where most of your referrals are going to come from.

Resources

If you are seeking more knowledge when it comes to the keywords that will do you best, you are going to have access to use resources like:

- Wordtracker's Free Basic Keyword Demand
- Moz Keyword Explorer
- Microsoft Bing Ads Intelligence
- Goodle AdWords Keyword Planner Tool

- Google Trends

Each of these resources are going to allow you to have a different perspective when it comes to the keywords and phrases that you choose to use on your site. Just be sure that you are using keywords that are going to pertain to the product that you are affiliated with.

Keyword Difficulty

So, that you can know which set of words are going to do the targeting properly, you must not only be aware of the need for every word and expression, but also be prepared to put in the work that is going to be needed to raise you through the rankings.

If the bigger brands are taking up the top results when you first start, then you are going to be fighting a battle that is going to take many years of battling for you to rise to the top of the rankings list. This is why you need to be able to understand all of the keyword difficulties.

Chapter nine: SEOs

SEO means Search Engine Optimization. Even if you are new to SEOs or trying to learn more about the new searches, you will need to get the information that you need so that you can deal with SEOs properly.

What is SEO?

SEO is a disciple that is going to focus on the visibility of your site in an organic search. An organic search is going to be the searches that you do not pay for. The SEO is going to encompass creative and technical elements that are going to help you in traffic increases, rising through the rankings, and an awareness of your site through search engines.

SEOs have many different aspects. They are going to be related to how other sites are linked to yours, the words that you place on your page, and how your site is structured. It has to be structured in the way that is going to cause it to be understood by a search engine.

SEOs are not just about building a website that is search engine friendly, but it is about making your site better for the people that are going to visit it.

SEO and your website

Most of the traffic that you find on the web is going to be driven through the major search engines such as Google and Bing. But, social media does its fair share of generating traffic to your website. Search engines are the main method for how most internet users look for things. It does not matter what your affiliated with, it will be able to be found through a search engine through just a few key phrases or words strung together.

Since search engines are rather difficult to understand in exactly how they are able to direct traffic to its intended target, they are going to act as a road to make this possible. When a search engine cannot find your website, or even add the content that you have on your site to its database, then you are going to be missing out on the traffic that could be driven to your site.

Search queries are going to be what a user inputs into a box on a search engine so that they can find what it is that they are looking for. Past experience has proven that the traffic from a search has the ability to make or break a website and its intended success. The targeted traffic is going to give a website a lot of revenue exposure, and publicity like no other channel is going to give. When you establish a SEO, you are going to be getting a better rate of return over the promotion that you are going to be able to achieve on your own.

Search engines and SEO

A search engine may not be a human, but it is still pretty smart granted it has the proper help. All of the major engines are going to continue to improve based on the technology of the web because of the results from users. But, search engines still have their limits on how they are able to operate.

The proper SEO is going to be able to give you hundreds if not thousands of people who are directed to your site. But, if you make one wrong move, you are going to end up hiding or even burying your search results so that your visibility is lost on a search engine.

As well as making your content more visible to search engines, SEOs help to boost your rankings so that you can be found easier by potential customers. Each and every day the internet becomes more competitive and you should be willing to perform and SEO so that you are able to take advantage of any visitors and customers for your product that you are affiliated with.

Am I able to do SEOs myself?

With SEOs being complex, you are going to be able to understand the very basics of an SEO. But, it does not matter how much knowledge you are able to retain, then you are going to be able to make a difference for your site. SEO education can be found across the web in multiple guides.

Take what you learn along with practice is going to help you in becoming a guru. If you are willing to learn and practice, then you are going to be able to grasp the core concepts of an SEO and do it yourself.

Chapter ten: Building Your Email List

Your email list is going to be one of the most important tools that you will have. Even with that being said, your marketing base it going to go down every year since people opt out of emails, move to a different company, or abandon their emails for a new one.

But, it is your job to make sure that you get new contacts on your email list through marketing campaigns to ensure your numbers keep moving up.

Using email

- Create content that is remarkable. If your content is not amazing, then you are going to end up losing subscribers. But, if it is, then it is going may be forwarded to their family that are not on your list, therefore helping you to grow your list.

- Encourage sharing by including buttons like social sharing and email to a friend in your emails. Whenever you have a new approach to a fresh network, friends of subscribers may find that they want to sign up for your list. So, at the bottom of your emails, you should have a subscribe button so that they can opt in for your emails too.

- Promote contests online such as free giveaways where subscribers can sign up or submit their entry with their email.

- Create multiple subscription types so that you can target content to specific people. You are going to get more people to subscribe if they are able to get emails that are targeted to them.

- Reinvigorate you emails with opt in campaigns. If most of your list is dead, then create a campaign message that can be sent out to your old list to encourage people to opt back in for your emails, this is going to help to remove any people that do not respond.

- Add in a link for your employee signature so that there is a landing page where they can sign up for your emails

New Content

- Create new lead gen offers such as ebooks that requires visitors to put their email in before they can download it.

- Create fee online tools where users can sign up by using their emails.

Social media

- Promote offers through Twitter campaigns

- Facebook pages can also be used to promote offers that can only be redeemed with an email address. These offers can be posted to your timeline and will include social sharing buttons.

- Call to action buttons can be activated at the top of your Facebook business page. The call to action button is going to take the user to a landing page that will require them to enter an email address.

- Publish links that are going to have offers posted on LinkedIn Company pages or other group discussions that are relevant to what you are promoting.

- Pinterest is growing every day and offers can be pinned to your board with a picture that will entice the reader to sign up with their email address.

- Add call to action buttons and URLs in your videos that are going to encourage people to subscribe to your email list.

- Promote offers and email sign ups through Google plus pages.

On your website

- Put offers that are only valid with email signups on your website. People should not have to dig around to maybe stumble across your subscription button. Offers should be kept up front and have call to action buttons on all of your pages.

- Whenever you have a guest on your blog, you should make call to action buttons for links so that your readers can subscribe to your blog in the author byline

With partners

- Run different promotions that are going to be on your partner's website or on their email list so that you can target new audience members from a fresh source.

- Host a marketing offer with your partner so that registration requires an email.

Traditional marketing/ advertising

- Get emails from events offline such as trade shows so that you can put them into your email database.

- Hose your own offline shows such as conferences or just meetups.

- Encourage traditional marketing campaigns like direct mail so that they have the option to receive email communications instead of snail mail.

- Host a webinar and when people register, collect their emails.

- Pay for search ads with a link on your landing page so that they can sign up for your emails.

- QR codes can be print marketing as well that can be scanned by a smart phone and lead someone to sign up for your email.

Chapter eleven: Registering a Domain Name and Maintaining It

Whenever you register a domain, you are taking the first step that is needed to establish your presence online. When you create and register your domain, you need to be able to avoid some of the mistakes that people tend to make while you choose the best domain name so that your site is reached but the appropriate audience and the most people possible.

Registering a domain with a hosting service

- First you need to choose what your preferred route is. No matter what, your site will be composed of multiple files which is going to result in you needing a place to store those files. You can store them in your own computer which is not going to require that you have a hosting service, or you can store them in a company server which is going to result in you having a hosting service. Most of the webhosting servers out there are going to allow you to register a domain name.

- If you decide to go with a host service, then you need to choose which service you want to use. Do your research to find the one that offers you the services that you want, but be sure to choose a reputable one.

- Many sites are going to have a place where you can check to see if the domain name that you want to use is available or not. If it is not, they are going to offer you some alternatives and if there is a cheaper domain with a different name, they will offer you that choice as well.

- Once you have found a domain name that you want, you are going to need to follow the instructions that services needs you to go through so that you can select your host name. You will also be offered the opportunity to add in other services that the host is going to provide.

- Fill out all of the forms that are necessary. It is going to include information about yourself so that the database knows who you are.

- You will need to purchase your domain name. Be sure that your payment is correct or you are not going to get your domain.

- Use the tools that they provide so that you can get your site up and running.

Without a hosting service

- Make sure that your internet service provider allows for you to host your own site. Some ISP will not allow this and will block your traffic to your site. If you need to do something special in order to get your ISP to grant you access to host your site, then do it. If they will not allow it at all, change ISP or select a different method of hosting.

- Chose where you want to register. You can choose a major hosting service, or find a website that is going to allow registration. You can also register a domain with a hosting company but you do not have to host with them. Just find one that is reputable. But, keep in mind that there are some hosts and registrars that are only going to allow you register certain top level domains.

- Get a server that is going to host our site. You have the option of repurposing an old computer or getting a server, just choose the one that is going to best suit your needs. But, be sure that it can also handle the needs of your site.

- You are going to need an IP address that is going to stay static. Most of the time IPs change, and if yours changes, then your site will not be able to be found.

- There is software that you have to have to run your server properly. There are a several different software programs available and you should choose the one that you are going to be eager to learn.

- Your router and your firewall are going to need to be reconfigured after you have gotten your server set up the way that you want it to be. The router will need to be forwarded correctly with the proper connections and the firewall needs to allow site traffic through.

- Once everything is set up correctly, your domain traffic is going to be sent to your site. You can test it after you are done on your own computer and then at a different location such as a friends house just to ensure that it works.

- When you run your own server, you are going to be at risk for some serious security holes. Your server is going to be easier to hack and it is up to you to make sure that you have the appropriate security precautions in place to prevent this from happening. Pay attention to your site and if there is a breach in security, fix it right away.

Maintaining your domain

Now that you own a website, you are going to need to keep the website up to date. All websites have to monitored so that any security breaches can be taken care of immediately.

- Fix broken links. When a link is broken, it is going to lead to nowhere. Basically, they are error pages. When a website has multiple pages, it has to be monitored for broken links. You can do this with tools that you are going to have access to with your host site. Once you find broken links, you should immediately fix them.

- An httaccess file is going to have several different functions. One of its main functions pertains to traffic and where it goes on your website. Once you have put an httaccess file in, you are going to be allowed to direct people to a www or non www page. But, all of your web traffic is going to be directed to a uniformed URL. This will increase the SEO trends of your page.

- Malware is software that is going to contaminate a computer. It is usually place d in your website by hackers. There are tools such as google webmaster to send notifications to you whenever there has been malware spotted on your site. Webmasters are going to need to check for malware and remove them with a high priority basis.

- A crawl error or a URL that has been blocked is going to stop a page from getting to the search engines. Therefore the page is not going to be visible to your readers. Google webmaster tools are going to tell you the crawl errors that are listed on your website so that they can be fixed and tracked for updates.

- Robot.txt files are going to help to notify when robots form search engines are found on the pages of your site that you are wanting them to not visit. This text will be helpful in blocking the indexing from any pages that are generated for search results inside of your website when there is no need for them to be indexed.

Chapter twelve: Engaging Readers

Writing your blog is not all about what you write, publish, promote. It is about creating a community so that your blog is a place that people are going to want to come back to and see what you are promoting. In order to build a better blog, you have to make it exciting.

Awesome articles

Your content is what readers come to see. If there are not articles about the products that you are affiliated with that are of interest, then you are not going to have a lot of readers. You have to attract readers to your articles. Inspire them to want to buy the product that you are trying to promote.

When you write articles that guide people to do things, then you are going to be inspiring your reader to do that. You are also going to be able to engage readers by motivating them. If you add in your own experiences, then your readers are more likely to read everything that you have to say.

Blog design

Design is just equally important just like your writing is. When your page is well designed, is it going to attract more people. Your design should be professional yet simple so that you do not overwhelming your readers with a bunch of designs that distract from your content. If you do not want to do the design yourself, then you are going to be able to hire a designer to design your site for you. When a blog is well designed, then the readers are going to stay on your site for longer.

Headlines

What you title your posts is going to attract readers or not. If you make your titles bold and exciting a reader is more than likely going to click on it to see what you are talking about. For example, if you were to see the word Killer! then you would click on it to see what they were talking about.

Headlines such as this can also be used on social media in order to get the word out more. When you write a great headline it is going to get more eyes than if you were to just put a simple headline that was not attractive.

Titles should be ten to twelve words so that you can add keywords into your title. You should think about detailing all of your headlines for all of your articles. Doing this is going to assist in describing what the article is going to be about.

Showcase

It is going to be easy to get people to your blog, but it is not easy to keep them there. Place your best post up front so that your visitors are able to look at those articles too. You are able to do this with things like a sidebar. You can also put your articles into categories to help your reader in their browsing.

Stay in touch

Have RSS feeds on your blog with the button located at the top of your blog. Also add in the options for email, Facebook, or whatever other social media that you are located on. These options are going to help to keep your readers connected. Eventually you are going to transform a visitor into a daily reader through RSS.

Show off your readers

Your readers need to get credit for even helping make your blog a possibility. Facebook widgets are available to help show off your different readers so that they can feel appreciated. Put your RSS counter on your blog so that others know that they are not the only one who is reading your blog. There are a few blog platforms that enable you to add a followers widget. But, this should only be added if you have a good number of followers, which should be more than a hundred.

Connection

Do not keep who you are a secret from your readers. Make it easy for your readers to connect with you on a personal level. If you communicate with your readers, they are going to come back on a regular basis thus creating a long term relationship between you and them. Show off all of your social buttons so that you can attract more people to connect with you.

Comments

Allow your readers to leave comments on your posts about what they think about what you wrote. If someone leaves a comment for you, always go in and reply to them thanking them, or answering any questions that they may have. Comments are going to help in boosting your returning readers.

Chat widgets can also be added to your blog to encourage interaction. Show off recent comments so that you can get more comments on your blog. Recent comments can also be added to your sidebar with a widget.

Give them a reason

Do not put everything that you know in your article. Leave some of it out so that your readers ask questions that you are able to reply to. If they have experiences with the product that you are selling, then you should encourage them to leave their experience for others to read and for you to see. Also do not forget to ask them to promote your posts to help you in promoting the product you are affiliated with.

Conclusion

Thank for making it through to the end of *Work from Home*, let's hope it was informative and able to provide you with all of the tools you need to achieve your goals whatever it may be.

The next step is to find your niche and start your business in affiliate marketing. It is not going to be simple, but it will be something that you are going to appreciate in the end.

You need to remember that you need to be patient. You are not going to get rich off of affiliate marketing overnight. It is going to take a lot of hard work and patience but you can do it!

Finally, if you found this book useful in anyway, a review on Amazon is always appreciated!

Great experience is shared on this very website:

www.lacobizonlinebusiness.com

www.ingramcontent.com/pod-product-compliance
Lightning Source LLC
Chambersburg PA
CBHW061225180526
45170CB00003B/1161